LE CORDON BLEU

HOME COLLECTION

·BISCUITS·

MURDOCH BOOKS®
Sydney • London • Vancouver • New York

contents

recipe ratings ❋ *easy* ❋❋ *a little more care needed* ❋❋❋ *more care needed*

Melting moments

As their name suggests, these melt-in-the-mouth biscuits with their soft butter cream and jam filling are simply irresistible.

*Preparation time **45 minutes***
*Total cooking time **20 minutes per tray***
Makes about 30

250 g (8 oz) unsalted butter, at room temperature
100 g (3¼ oz) icing sugar, sifted
1 teaspoon finely grated lemon rind
2 egg yolks
300 g (10 oz) plain flour
2 tablespoons raspberry jam, beaten
icing sugar, to dust

BUTTER CREAM
80 g (2¾ oz) caster sugar
1 egg white
80 g (2¾ oz) unsalted butter, at room temperature

1 Preheat the oven to moderate 180°C (350°F/Gas 4). Brush two baking trays with melted butter. Using a wooden spoon or an electric whisk, cream together the butter, icing sugar and lemon rind until light and fluffy.
2 Add the egg yolks and mix thoroughly. Sift in the flour and work with a wooden spoon until the mixture comes together to form a smooth soft paste. Spoon into a piping bag with an 8 mm (¹/3 inch) star nozzle.
3 Pipe enough 1.5–2 cm (⁵/8–3/4 inch) rosettes to fill the prepared baking trays, spacing well apart (see Chef's techniques, page 63). Bake for 10–12 minutes, or until the edges are golden. Cool on a wire rack. Repeat with the remaining mixture, preparing the trays as instructed in step 1.
4 To make the butter cream, in a small saucepan, over low heat, dissolve 60 g (2 oz) of the sugar in 1 tablespoon water, stirring occasionally. Increase the heat and bring to the boil. Simmer, without stirring, for 3–5 minutes. To prevent crystals of sugar forming, wipe down the sides of the pan with a brush dipped in water. Meanwhile, whisk the egg white until stiff. Add the remaining caster sugar and whisk until stiff and shiny and peaks form when the whisk is lifted. While whisking the meringue, pour on the bubbling syrup in a thin steady stream, aiming between the bowl and the whisk. Continue to whisk until the mixture is cold. Gradually add the soft butter.
5 Divide the biscuits into pairs and spread jam on the flat side of one of each pair. Using a plain 4 mm (¹/4 inch) nozzle, pipe a little butter cream onto the other biscuit, sandwich the two together and dust lightly with sifted icing sugar.

Florentines

Accredited to Austrian bakers, this wonderful mixture of sugar, butter, cream,
nuts and fruit has its origins in Italy. Crisp to eat, they have the added allure of a
chocolate base, which is optional though traditional.

*Preparation time **20 minutes + 10 minutes standing***
*Total cooking time **15 minutes per tray***
Makes 25–30

120 g (4 oz) unsalted butter
125 g (4 oz) caster sugar
100 g (3¹/4 oz) candied orange peel, finely chopped or
***   mixed peel***
30 g (1 oz) glacé cherries, cut into 8 pieces
60 g (2 oz) blanched flaked almonds
120 g (4 oz) blanched almonds, chopped
30 ml (1 fl oz) thick (double) cream
250 g (8 oz) good-quality dark chocolate, chopped

1 Preheat the oven to moderate 180°C (350°F/Gas 4).
Brush two baking trays with melted butter.
2 Melt the butter in a small saucepan, stir in the sugar,
slowly bring to the boil and remove from the heat. Add
the candied peel, cherries, the flaked and chopped
almonds and mix well. Whisk the cream until it is thick
and gently stir it into the warm mixture. Set aside for
about 10 minutes, or until cool and thick.
3 Using a heaped teaspoon of mixture for each
Florentine, spoon on enough mounds of the mixture to
fill the two baking trays (see Chef's techniques, page
63). Space well apart as the biscuits will spread. Bake for
about 5 minutes, or until lightly set. Using a large cutter
or a cup, shape the spread mixture into neat rounds by
pulling in the edges. Return to the oven for 4 minutes.
Reshape with the cutter and leave to cool for 3 minutes,
or until firm enough to remove from the tray. Carefully
lift them with a palette knife and cool on a wire rack.
Repeat with the remaining mixture, preparing the trays
as instructed in step 1. Warm the mixture a little if it has
cooled too much to spoon easily.
4 Bring a pan half-full of water to the boil, then remove
from the heat. Place the chocolate in a heatproof bowl
and place over the pan of steaming water, without
touching the water. Stir occasionally until the chocolate
has melted and leave to cool to room temperature.
Using a palette knife, spread on to the smooth underside
of the Florentines. Return to the rack until the chocolate
is just setting. Run a fork through the chocolate to make
wavy lines and leave to set at room temperature.

Chef's tip Florentines make excellent petits fours if
made with ¹/2 teaspoon of mixture. They will store in an
airtight containter for up to 1 week. Any extra raw
mixture can be stored in the refrigerator for 1 week.

English rout biscuits

These decorative biscuits are excellent served with tea, coffee or even a glass of wine.

Preparation time **15 minutes + drying overnight**
Total cooking time **10 minutes**
Makes about 24

50 g (1³/4 oz) semolina or ground rice
120 g (4 oz) ground almonds
120 g (4 oz) icing sugar
¹/4 teaspoon ground cinnamon
1 egg white
halved glacé cherries or halved almonds, to decorate
50 g (1³/4 oz) apricot jam

1 Sprinkle two baking trays with the semolina or ground rice. Sift the almonds, sugar and cinnamon into a bowl. Add the egg white and mix to a very stiff paste.
2 Spoon the mixture into a piping bag. Using a large star nozzle, pipe the mixture onto the prepared baking trays in rosettes 3 cm (1¹/4 inch) wide or 'fleurs-de-lys' 3 cm (1¹/4 inch) long (see Chef's techniques, page 63). Place half a glacé cherry or half an almond in the centre of each biscuit to decorate. Leave uncovered overnight to dry .
3 Preheat the oven to very hot 240°C (475°F/Gas 9). Bake for 8–10 minutes, or until the biscuits are just browned on the edges.
4 Place the jam in a small saucepan with 1 tablespoon water until melted. Sieve and brush over the biscuits.

Chef's tips The mixture should be very stiff and even difficult to pipe to obtain a crisp, dry result.

A 'fleur-de-lys' is a heraldic symbol, and the shape represents a lily, with its three distinct petals.

Sugar cookies

Whether flavoured with almond, vanilla, cinnamon or lemon, these sugar-coated biscuits are always popular. This practical recipe allows you to freeze leftover dough, thus enabling you to produce freshly made biscuits within minutes for unexpected visitors.

Preparation time **15 minutes + 25 minutes refrigeration**
Total cooking time **15 minutes per tray**
Makes 45

200 g (6¹/2 oz) plain flour
pinch of salt
2 teaspoons baking powder
115 g (3³/4 oz) unsalted butter, at room temperature
225 g (7¹/4 oz) caster sugar
I egg, lightly beaten
¹/4 teaspoon almond essence
60 g (2 oz) demerara sugar

1 Sift together the flour, salt and baking powder. In a bowl, beat the butter with a wooden spoon or electric beaters until smooth. Add the sugar gradually to the butter, beating continuously until pale and creamy. Pour in the egg, a little at a time, beating well after each addition. Stir in the almond essence.
2 Add the flour to the butter mixture and mix well. Cover the dough with plastic wrap and place in the refrigerator to chill for about 15 minutes, or until firm.
3 Once the mixture is firm, shape it into a long roll about 5 cm (2 inches) in diameter. Roll the dough in plastic wrap, twisting the ends to seal well. Return the dough to the refrigerator for a further 10 minutes. Unwrap and roll the dough in the demerara sugar until the outside is well coated, but the ends are clean. Refrigerate until needed.
4 Preheat the oven to moderate 180°C (350°F/Gas 4). Brush two baking trays with melted butter. Slice enough of the chilled roll into rounds 5 mm (1/4 inch) thick to fill the baking trays. Place on the prepared baking tray, 4 cm (1¹/2 inches) apart. Refrigerate the rest of the mixture. Bake for about 12–15 minutes, or until golden, then transfer to a wire rack to cool. Repeat with the remaining mixture, preparing the trays with melted butter as instructed above.

Chef's tips As an alternative to almond essence, flavour the dough with vanilla essence, cinnamon or finely grated lemon rind. You could also roll the dough in coloured sugar crystals intead of demerara sugar.

This dough freezes wonderfully for up to 4 weeks. Place in the freezer when the dough is shaped in a long roll. When you want to use it, simply slice the frozen dough into rounds using a serrated bread knife. The biscuits can be cooked from frozen, but they may need a few minutes longer in the oven.

Orange tuiles

The delicious orange, almond and Grand Marnier flavour of these delicate crisp biscuits make them a perfect accompaniment to vanilla ice cream or a fresh fruit sorbet.

Preparation time **15 minutes**
Total cooking time **5 minutes per tray**
Makes 60

70 ml (2¼ fl oz) orange juice
finely grated rind of 1 orange
50 ml (1¾ fl oz) Grand Marnier
250 g (8 oz) caster sugar
100 g (3¼ oz) unsalted butter, melted but cooled
200 g (6½ oz) almonds, finely chopped
125 g (4 oz) plain flour

1 Preheat the oven to moderately hot 190°C (375°F/Gas 5). Brush two baking trays with melted butter and refrigerate.
2 Place the orange juice and rind, Grand Marnier and sugar in a bowl. Stir in the melted butter, chopped almonds and flour.
3 Prepare the tuiles following the method in the Chef's techniques on page 63. Bake one tray of tuiles at a time for 5 minutes, or until lightly golden all over. Repeat with the remaining mixture, preparing the trays as instructed in step 1.

Chef's tip The tuiles can be stored in an airtight container for up to a week.

Coconut tuiles

'Tuile' is the French word for tile. These biscuits are shaped to represent the slightly rounded, overlapping tiles found on many European roofs, especially around the Mediterranean.

Preparation time **15 minutes**
Total cooking time **5 minutes per tray**
Makes 40

3 small egg whites
80 g (2¾ oz) desiccated coconut
100 g (3¼ oz) caster sugar
20 g (¾ oz) plain flour
70 g (2¼ oz) unsalted butter, melted, but cooled

1 Preheat the oven to moderately hot 190°C (375°F/Gas 5). Brush two baking trays with melted butter and refrigerate.
2 Lightly beat the egg whites with a fork to loosen them. Add the coconut, caster sugar, flour and butter and stir together.
3 Prepare the tuiles following the method in the Chef's techniques on page 63. Bake one tray of tuiles at a time for 5 minutes, or until lightly golden all over. Repeat with the remaining mixture, preparing the trays as instructed in step 1.

Chef's tips To make almond tuiles, use 80 g (2¾ oz) finely chopped almonds in place of the coconut.

The tuiles can be stored in an airtight container for up to a week.

Orange tuiles (top) and Coconut tuiles

Sablés nantais

*Generally round with fluted edges, these golden crumbly biscuits melt in the mouth. It is due
to this delicate crumbly texture that these biscuits from the French region of Nantes are called sablés,
from the French word 'sable', meaning sand.*

*Preparation time **15 minutes + 1 hour 20 minutes**
  refrigeration*
*Total cooking time **12 minutes per tray***
Makes about 50

200 g (6¹/2 oz) unsalted butter, at room temperature
200 g (6¹/2 oz) icing sugar
1 egg, lightly beaten
4 egg yolks
2 teaspoons vanilla extract or essence
400 g (12³/4 oz) plain flour
pinch of salt
¹/2 teaspoon baking powder
pinch of ground cinnamon
two drops coffee essence

1 Preheat the oven to moderately hot 190°C
(375°F/Gas 5). Brush two baking trays with melted
butter and refrigerate.
2 Using a wooden spoon or electric whisk, cream
together the butter and the sugar. Mix together half of
the beaten egg with the egg yolks and reserve the
remaining half egg. Gradually add the egg yolk mixture
to the butter mixture, beating well after each addition.

Stir in the vanilla.
3 Sift the flour, salt, baking powder and cinnamon
together and fold into the butter mixture. Using a
spatula, scrape the mixture onto a large piece of plastic
wrap, pat lightly to flatten. Wrap and refrigerate for at
least 1 hour.
4 In a small bowl, lightly beat the remaining ¹/2 egg
with the coffee essence and set aside.
5 Roll out the pastry to a 3–4 mm (¹/8–¹/4 inch)
thickness between two sheets of baking paper (see
Chef's techniques, page 63). Cut out enough shapes
using a 5 cm (2 inch) round fluted cutter to fill the two
baking trays, then return the remaining mixture to the
refrigerator. Place the shapes on the baking trays and
chill in the refrigerator for about 20 minutes. Brush with
the egg and coffee essence mixture. Using a fork, make
crisscross patterns on top of the biscuits. Bake for about
12 minutes, or until golden. Remove from the baking
trays and cool on a wire rack. Repeat with the remaining
mixture, preparing the trays as instructed in step 1.

Chef's tip The buttery pastry will soften quickly in a
warm kitchen. Roll out in batches to keep the pastry
cool and easy to work with. Sablés nantais will keep,
stored in an airtight container, for up to 1 week.

Rum and raisin biscuits

The classic combination of rum and raisins gives excellent results in these thin crisp biscuits.
Delicious with a cup of tea or coffee, or served with vanilla ice cream.

*Preparation time **15 minutes + 1 hour soaking***
*Total cooking time **7 minutes per tray***
Makes about 25

30 g (1 oz) raisins, chopped (see Chef's tip)
40 ml (1¼ fl oz) rum
50 g (1¾ oz) unsalted butter, at room temperature
40 g (1¼ oz) icing sugar
2–3 drops vanilla extract or essence
1 egg, lightly beaten
50 g (1¾ oz) plain flour

1 Place the raisins in a small bowl, pour over the rum, cover with plastic wrap. Leave to soak for at least 1 hour. Preheat the oven to moderately hot 190°C (375°F/ Gas 5). Brush two baking trays with softened butter, then refrigerate until set. Brush the tray with some more butter to make a double coating and refrigerate again.
2 In a large bowl, soften the butter using a wooden spoon or an electric whisk. Gradually beat in the icing sugar, then continue to beat until the mixture is light and fluffy. Add the vanilla. Gradually add the egg to the butter mixture, beating well after each addition to prevent curdling or separation.
3 Sift the flour and add it to the butter mixture, beating well until smooth. Stir in the soaked, chopped raisins and rum and mix well.
4 Spoon the mixture into a piping bag fitted with a 1 cm (½ inch) plain nozzle. Pipe enough 2.5 cm (1 inch) wide rounds to fill the two prepared baking trays, spacing them at least 3 cm (1¼ inches) apart as they will spread during baking.
5 To encourage the biscuits to spread, bang the trays heavily once on the work surface. Bake for 6–7 minutes, or until golden brown at the edges, but slightly paler in the centre. Remove from the trays and transfer to a wire rack to cool. Repeat with the remaining mixture, preparing the trays as instructed in step 1.

Chef's tips If you find the raisins stick to the knife when chopping, add a little flour from the recipe as you chop.

As a variation, add 10 g (¼ oz) chopped angelica and glacé cherries for a colourful jewel-like biscuit.

Eponges

The name 'éponge', meaning sponge in French, was probably given to these almond-flavoured biscuits because of their resemblance to sea sponges. The crunchy almond coating provides a good contrast to the light meringue texture of these petits fours biscuits.

*Preparation time **20 minutes***
*Total cooking time **10 minutes***
Makes about 20

2 egg whites
25 g (³/4 oz) caster sugar
50 g (1³/4 oz) icing sugar
50 g (1³/4 oz) blanched almonds, ground
150 g (5 oz) almonds, finely chopped
75 g (2¹/2 oz) seedless raspberry jam
icing sugar, to dust

1 Preheat the oven to moderately hot 190°C (375°F/Gas 5). Brush two baking trays with melted butter, sprinkle with flour and tap off the excess.
2 Whisk the egg whites and a pinch of the caster sugar with a balloon whisk or electric whisk for 2 minutes, or until soft peaks form. Slowly add the remaining caster sugar, whisking well after each addition. Sift the icing sugar and ground almonds together and fold in until well mixed. Spoon the mixture into a piping bag fitted with a 1 cm (1/2 inch) plain round nozzle. Pipe small, evenly spaced 3 cm (11/4 inch) wide, domed rounds onto the prepared baking trays. Sprinkle with the chopped almonds and bake for 7–10 minutes, or until golden. Remove from the tray and cool on a wire rack.
3 When cool, arrange the éponges, flat-side-up, in pairs. On one of the pair, pipe or spread a little jam and sandwich with the other. Sprinkle with sifted icing sugar.

Chef's tip If you are cooking more than one tray of biscuits in a non-convection oven, swap them around halfway through cooking to ensure even baking.

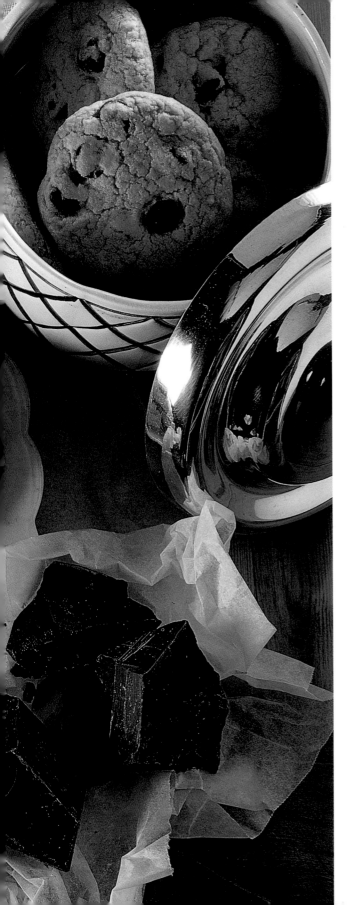

Chocolate chip cookies

These cookies, originally created at the Toll House Inn in Massachusetts in the 1920's, became so popular that small round chocolate pieces, known as 'chips', were marketed especially for them.

Preparation time **20 minutes**
Total cooking time **20 minutes per tray**
Makes 24

115 g (3³/4 oz) unsalted butter, at room temperature
100 g (3¹/4 oz) soft brown sugar
100 g (3¹/4 oz) caster sugar
1 egg, lightly beaten
¹/4 teaspoon vanilla extract or essence
155 g (5 oz) plain flour
pinch of baking powder
100 g (3¹/4 oz) ground almonds
150 g (5 oz) chocolate chips

1 Preheat the oven to moderate 180°C (350°F/Gas 4). Brush two baking trays with melted butter and refrigerate until set.
2 Using a wooden spoon or an electric whisk, cream the butter and sugars until light and fluffy. Gradually add the egg and vanilla, beating well after each addition.
3 Sift the flour, baking powder and ground almonds together. Fold half into the creamed mixture. When almost incorporated, add the rest of the sifted mixture, then add the chocolate chips as you fold.
4 Divide into 24 portions and roll into balls. Place the balls, spaced well apart, on the two prepared trays and flatten lightly. Bake for 15–20 minutes, or until golden brown. Remove from the tray while still hot and transfer to a cooling rack. Repeat with the remaining mixture, preparing the trays as instructed in step 1. Store in an airtight container.

Macaroons

These vanilla-flavoured macaroons, crisp on the outside with surprisingly soft, moist centres, can be sandwiched together with different flavoured fillings, such as fruit jams or melted chocolate.

Preparation time **15 minutes**
Total cooking time **20 minutes per tray**
Makes 40

125 g (4 oz) ground almonds
250 g (8 oz) icing sugar
4 egg whites
2–3 drops vanilla extract or essence
pinch of caster sugar
125 g (4 oz) dark chocolate

1 Place two baking trays together and line the top tray with baking paper (this double thickness tray will prevent the bottom of the macaroons overbrowning during cooking). Preheat the oven to warm 160°C (315°F/Gas 2–3).
2 Sift the almonds and icing sugar into a bowl, then sift them again to make sure that they are thoroughly mixed. In a separate bowl, whisk the egg whites and vanilla with a pinch of caster sugar until stiff and shiny

and the mixture forms peaks when the whisk is lifted.
3 Using a metal spoon, gently fold the dry ingredients into the egg white, trying not to lose any air. The mixture should be shiny and soft, not liquid.
4 Spoon into a piping bag fitted with a 7.5 mm (1/4 inch) nozzle. Pipe enough 3 cm (1 1/4 inch) wide rounds to fill the prepared tray, leaving a little space between them. Bake for about 15–20 minutes, or until golden and crisp, checking the macaroons frequently during cooking. Cool on the tray for a few minutes, then remove to a wire rack. Repeat with the remaining mixture, preparing the trays as instructed in step 1.
5 Half-fill a pan with water and bring to the boil. Remove from the heat. Place the chocolate in a heatproof bowl and set over the steaming water. Stir until the chocolate melts. Sandwich the macaroons together in pairs using the chocolate and leave to cool.

Chef's tip If you are cooking more than one tray of biscuits in a non-convection oven, swap them around halfway through cooking to ensure even baking.

Lunettes

'Lunettes' is the French word for spectacles. Made to represent spectacles,
these biscuits are elegant for tea time, but also fun for children.

*Preparation time **30 minutes + 30 minutes refrigeration***
*Total cooking time **10 minutes per tray***
Makes 10

45 g (1¹/2 oz) ground almonds
110 g (3³/4 oz) plain flour
45 g (1¹/2 oz) unsalted butter
1 teaspoon finely grated lemon rind
45 g (1¹/2 oz) caster sugar
¹/2 egg, beaten
50 g (1³/4 oz) apricot jam
icing sugar, to dust
60 g (2 oz) raspberry jam

1 Preheat the oven to moderate 180°C (350°F/Gas 4). Brush two baking trays with melted butter and dust lightly with flour. Sift together the almonds and flour.
2 Using a wooden spoon or electric beaters, cream together the butter, lemon rind and sugar until light and fluffy. Add the egg, a little at a time, beating well after each addition. Add the flour and almonds and stir together to form a rough dough. Draw together by hand to form a ball, wrap in plastic wrap, flatten slightly and refrigerate for about 30 minutes. Roll out the dough between two sheets of baking paper to about a 3 mm (¹/8 inch) thickness (see Chef's techniques, page 63).
3 Using an 8 cm (3 inch) oval cutter, cut out about 20 biscuits and transfer as many as will fit comfortably to the prepared trays. Using a 1–1.5 cm (¹/2–⁵/8 inch) round cutter, or the end of a 1 cm (¹/2 inch) piping nozzle, cut out two holes from half of the oval biscuits. These will become the tops of the lunettes. Refrigerate the rest of the dough until needed.
4 Bake for 10 minutes, or until light golden. While still warm, remove the biscuits from the trays to a wire rack. Repeat with the remaining mixture, preparing the trays as instructed in step 1.
5 Warm the apricot jam, brush over the base of the whole biscuits and sandwich together with a biscuit with holes in the top.
6 Dust with sifted icing sugar. Beat the raspberry jam in a bowl until it flows. Fill a piping bag fitted with a 4 mm (¹/4 inch) plain nozzle and fill in each of the holes on the sandwiched biscuits with the jam. If you don't have a piping bag, drop the jam from the tip of a teaspoon.

Shortbread

Shortbread can be made with plain flour alone, however the texture is greatly enhanced by using a combination of flours. Adding rice flour produces a light result, while semolina will give a crunchy texture.

Preparation time **10 minutes + 10 minutes refrigeration**
Total cooking time **25 minutes**
Makes 8

120 g (4 oz) unsalted butter, at room temperature
60 g (2 oz) caster sugar
120 g (4 oz) plain flour
60 g (2 oz) rice flour or fine semolina, sifted twice
1¹/2 tablespoons caster sugar, for dusting

1 Preheat the oven to moderate 180°C (350°F/Gas 4). Beat the butter in a wide bowl until smooth. Gradually beat in the sugar. Add the plain flour and rice flour or semolina and stir with a knife until well blended.
2 Press the mixture into an 18 cm (7 inch) round shallow tin with a removable base. Make sure that the mixture is level and prick the surface evenly with a fork. Place in the refrigerator to chill for 10 minutes.
3 Sprinkle the surface of the shortbread with the extra caster sugar and bake for 25 minutes, or until golden.
4 While the shortbread is still hot, carefully remove the outer tin, and cut into eight wedges using a large sharp knife. Don't separate the pieces as this will make them dry out. After 5 minutes, the shortbread will be firmer—transfer to a wire rack and sprinkle with a little more caster sugar.

Chef's tips The shortbread may rise or wrinkle slightly during baking—this is quite normal.

The shortbread will keep for up to a week if stored in an airtight container or wrapped in foil.

Langues-de-chat

'Langue-de-chat', the French term for cat's tongue, is the name given to these biscuits due to their resemblance to the shape of a cat's tongue. Delicately flavoured, light and crisp, these biscuits may be served with a sweet soufflé or as an elegant accompaniment to coffee.

*Preparation time **15 minutes***
*Total cooking time **10 minutes per tray***
Makes about 50

100 g (3¼ oz) icing sugar
100 g (3¼ oz) unsalted butter, at room temperature
3–4 drops vanilla extract or essence
3 egg whites, lightly beaten
100 g (3¼ oz) plain flour

1 Preheat the oven to moderately hot 200°C (400°F/Gas 6). Brush two baking trays with melted butter and refrigerate.

2 Using a wooden spoon or electric beaters, cream the icing sugar and butter together. When the mixture is pale and light, beat in the vanilla.

3 Add the egg whites slowly, beating constantly and being careful not to allow the mixture to curdle. If it does, add a large pinch of the measured flour.

4 Sift the flour into the bowl, then using a large metal spoon or plastic spatula, gently fold the flour into the butter mixture, mixing lightly until combined. Spoon into a piping bag fitted with a 7 mm (1/3 inch) plain nozzle and pipe enough 8 cm (3 inch) lengths to fill the prepared baking trays. Leave at least 5 cm (2 inches) between the biscuits as they will spread during baking. Bake for 7–10 minutes, or until the edges are golden brown, but the centres yellow.

5 Use a palette knife or fish slice to remove the biscuits from the tray while they are still warm. If they cool and become too brittle to move, return them to the oven to warm for a moment or two. Repeat with the remaining mixture, preparing the trays as instructed in step 1.

Chef's tip Langues-de-chat may be used to line moulds that are then filled with light creamy mixtures such as mousses, chilled to set and turned out. Or they can be placed around the sides of cream coated cakes. Store in an airtight container for up to 2 weeks.

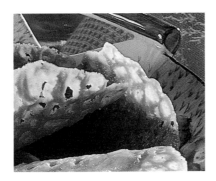

Ginger thins

Crisp, thin and lacy, these ginger-flavoured biscuits are delicious served with ice cream or light, creamy desserts.

Preparation time **10 minutes**
Total cooking time **10 minutes per tray**
Makes 12

15 g (¹/₂ oz) unsalted butter
15 g (¹/₂ oz) icing sugar
30 g (1 oz) golden syrup
20 g (³/₄ oz) plain flour
¹/₂ teaspoon ground ginger
pinch of salt

1 Brush two baking trays with melted butter and refrigerate until set. Brush once more with butter and refrigerate again. Preheat the oven to moderately hot 200°C (400°F/Gas 6). Cut a round 5 cm (2 inches) in diameter from the centre of a piece of plastic (a margarine tub lid is perfect). This will give you a plastic stencil with a 5 cm (2 inch) round hole in the centre.
2 In a pan, gently heat the butter, icing sugar and golden syrup, stirring until the sugar has dissolved. Remove from the heat and allow to cool slightly. Sift the flour, ginger and salt together twice and stir into the butter mixture.
3 Prepare the biscuits with the plastic stencil, following the method in the Chef's techniques on page 62.
4 Bake for 6–7 minutes, or until golden brown. Immediately lift the biscuits from the tray, and while still warm and pliable, shape over a rolling pin or roll them carefully around the rounded handle of a wooden spoon. Leave the shapes to cool on a wire rack. Repeat with the remaining mixture, preparing the trays as instructed in step 1. Warm the mixture a little if it has cooled too much to spoon easily. When cool, immediately place in an airtight container to prevent the biscuits going soggy.

Chef's tips If the biscuits set on the tray before you can lift them all off, return the tray to the oven to warm them through again.

Try cutting fancy shapes, such as a star or moon from the plastic for the stencil.

To make cinnamon thins, replace the ground ginger with ground cinnamon

Amaretti

Traditionally made with bitter almonds, this recipe uses the more readily available blanched almonds.

Preparation time **10 minutes**
Total cooking time **15 minutes per tray**
Makes about 40

75 g (2¹/₂ oz) blanched almonds, halved or chopped
75 g (2¹/₂ oz) caster sugar
1 egg white
3 teaspoons Amaretto liqueur
2 drops almond essence
icing sugar, to dust

1 Preheat the oven to moderate 180°C (350°F/Gas 4). Line two baking trays with baking paper.

2 Place the almonds and the sugar in a food processor and process to a fine powder. Add the egg white, Amaretto and almond essence and process to form a soft dough.

3 Spoon the mixture into a piping bag, fitted with a 1.5 cm (5/8 inch) plain nozzle. Pipe enough 2.5 cm (1 inch) rounds to fill the two prepared baking trays, spacing the biscuits well apart. Hold the nozzle 1 cm (1/2 inch) away from the tray to form well-rounded shapes. Bake for 12–15 minutes, or until golden. Cool on a wire rack. Repeat with the remaining mixture, preparing the trays as instructed in step 1. Dust with sifted icing sugar while still warm.

Chef's tips For a good result, make sure the almonds and sugar are very finely ground before adding the egg white.

To be traditionally Italian, place two biscuits flatside together and wrap in coloured tissue paper, twisting the ends. They look wonderful piled on a serving plate or given as gifts.

For a variation, top each biscuit with half an almond before baking.

Vanilla biscuits

These biscuits are traditionally served with a glass of sweet wine or Madeira. Enjoy them with tea or coffee or try them with mulled wine when the weather is cold. They are particularly good eaten with poached fruits served in their syrup.

Preparation time **20 minutes + 5 hours standing time**
Total cooking time **20 minutes**
Makes 40

65 g (2¼ oz) caster sugar
1 egg
1 egg yolk
2–3 drops vanilla extract or essence
1 teaspoon finely grated lemon rind
65 g (2¼ oz) plain flour
extra caster sugar, to dust

1 Line two baking trays with baking paper.
2 Half-fill a saucepan with water, bring it to the boil and remove from the heat. Meanwhile, put the sugar, egg, egg yolk, vanilla and lemon rind in a large bowl and place over the pan of steaming water. The base of the bowl should be just above the level of the water. Whisk with electric beaters for 5–10 minutes, or until the mixture becomes thick and mousse-like and leaves a trail as it falls from the whisk. Remove the bowl from the pan and continue to whisk for 5 minutes, or until the mixture is cold.
3 Sift the flour and fold it into the egg mixture. Use a metal spoon or plastic spatula and fold until just combined. Spoon the mixture into a piping bag fitted with a 2 cm (³/4 inch) plain nozzle and pipe rounded mounds of the mixture about 2 cm (1 inch) in diameter and spaced well apart onto the baking trays. Sprinkle with the extra caster sugar. Leave the mixture to dry on the baking trays for 4–5 hours at room temperature. Preheat the oven to slow 150°C (300°F/Gas 2).
4 Bake for 20 minutes, or until golden brown and firm to the touch. Transfer the biscuits to a wire rack to cool.

Chef's tip For a variation, you could sandwich two biscuits together using a little jam.

Lebkuchen

A traditional Austrian and German spicy soft biscuit that comes into its own in winter and especially for Christmas. Delicious served with tea, coffee or mulled wine in wintertime.

Preparation time **30 minutes**
Total cooking time **25 minutes**
Makes 24

40 g (1¼ oz) chopped mixed peel
155 g (5 oz) plain flour
large pinch of ground cloves
½ teaspoon ground cinnamon
½ teaspoon ground ginger
large pinch of ground nutmeg
¼ teaspoon baking powder
85 g (2¾ oz) ground almonds
1 egg
60 g (2 oz) soft dark brown sugar
180 ml (5¾ fl oz) clear honey
3 tablespoons milk
125 g (4 oz) icing sugar
1 teaspoon brandy

1 Preheat the oven to moderately hot 200°C (400°F/Gas 6). Brush a 20 x 30 cm (8 x 12 inch) swiss roll tin with melted butter, line the base with greaseproof paper and brush with butter. Dust the tin with flour, turning to coat the base and sides thoroughly.
2 Lightly dust a work surface with flour, place the mixed peel on it, toss lightly in the flour and then chop finely using a large sharp knife. The flour will stop the peel sticking to the knife. Sift the flour, cloves, cinnamon, ginger, nutmeg and baking powder into a large bowl. Add the mixed peel and stir in the almonds.

3 Place the egg and brown sugar in a bowl and whisk with an electric whisk until increased in volume and pale in colour. Whisk in the honey, then the milk. Pour onto the flour mixture and stir briskly until the mixture resembles a batter.
4 Pour the mixture into the tin and spread evenly to the corners. Bake on the middle shelf of the oven for about 20–25 minutes, or until just springy to the light touch of a finger. While the Lebkuchen is cooking, prepare the icing.
5 To make the icing, sift the icing sugar into a small bowl, add 1 tablespoon water and the brandy and mix with a wooden spoon to a thick coating consistency. It should run, but leave a trail as it falls back. If it doesn't fall from the spoon, it may need a little more water.
6 Loosen the sides of the Lebkuchen and turn it out of the tin onto a tray, then invert onto a wire rack, crust-side-up. Brush the top with the icing while it is still warm—it will run to give a thin glaze. Leave to cool and then cut into 8 slices lengthways and 3 across to make 24 pieces. Remove from the paper.

Chef's tips Lebkuchen may be served without icing. You can also cool them and then put on the icing very thinly, colouring small amounts of icing differently to give pink, white and yellow biscuits from the same batch. Or, perhaps dip the top of some into melted dark chocolate. A small sprinkling of tiny multicoloured hundreds and thousands are also traditional on the icing.

Lebkuchen will store in an airtight container, for at least 1 month.

Thumbprint cookies

The name given to these simple but delicious cookies comes from the method—after placing small balls of dough onto a baking tray, indentations are made with the thumb and then filled with jam.

Preparation time **35 minutes + 30 minutes refrigeration**
Total cooking time: **25 minutes per tray**
Makes about 36

250 g (8 oz) plain flour
1/4 teaspoon bicarbonate of soda
1/4 teaspoon salt
250 g (8 oz) unsalted butter, at room temperature
85 g (2 3/4 oz) icing sugar
l egg
l teaspoon vanilla extract or essence
200 g (6 1/2 oz) walnuts or almonds, chopped
raspberry jam

1 Preheat the oven to moderate 180°C (350°F/Gas 4). Brush two baking trays with melted butter.
2 Sift together the flour, bicarbonate of soda and salt. Cream together the butter and icing sugar until smooth and creamy. Add the egg and vanilla and beat well. Mix in the dry ingredients until completely blended. Cover and refrigerate for 30 minutes.
3 Scoop up heaped teaspoons of the dough and roll into balls about 2.5 cm (1 inch) in diameter. Roll the balls in the chopped nuts, pressing the nuts in well. Use enough pieces to fill the prepared baking sheets, spacing them about 5 cm (2 inches) apart. Press the centre of each ball with your thumb to make a deep impression. Using the handle of a spoon or a pastry bag fitted with a small plain nozzle, fill the impressions with the jam, being careful not to overfill.
4 Bake for 20–25 minutes, or until the nuts are toasted. Remove the biscuits from the baking trays and cool on a wire rack. Repeat with the remaining mixture, preparing the trays as instructed in step 1.

Chef's tips If you are cooking more than one tray of biscuits in a non-convection oven, swap them around halfway through cooking to ensure even baking.

Use a good-quality jam as it will hold well and give a better flavour and colour. You could also use different coloured jams, such as apricot or marmalade.

Biscotti

The name of these spicy little biscuits literally means 'twice baked'.
They are ideal served with ice cream, sorbet, warm fruit compote or even with a cup of coffee,
although they were traditionally served to be dipped into a glass of sweet wine.

Preparation time **25 minutes**
Total cooking time **1 hour 10 minutes**
Makes about **40**

3 eggs
275 g (9 oz) caster sugar
I teaspoon salt
I teaspoon vanilla extract or essence
finely grated rind of I orange
finely grated rind of I lemon
425 g (13¹/2 oz) plain flour
2 teaspoons baking powder
¹/2 teaspoon ground cloves
100 g (3¹/4 oz) blanched hazelnuts, lightly roasted and
 roughly chopped (see Chef's tips)
50 g (1³/4 oz) blanched whole almonds, lightly roasted
 and roughly chopped (see Chef's tips)
¹/2 egg, lightly beaten
100 g (3¹/4 oz) caster sugar, for rolling
2 teaspoons ground cloves, for rolling

1 Preheat the oven to warm 160°C (315°F/Gas 2–3). Brush a 20 cm (8 inch) square tin with melted butter, line the base with baking paper and coat the sides with a very thin layer of flour. Refrigerate until the butter has set. Fill a saucepan half full of water, bring to the boil and remove from the heat. Place the eggs, sugar, salt, vanilla and orange and lemon rind into a bowl. Place the bowl on the pan over, but not touching, the steaming water. Whisk until the mixture is thick and mousse-like, and a trail is left when the whisk is lifted. Remove the bowl and continue to whisk until the bowl feels cold and the mixture is cold, light and fluffy.

2 Sift together the flour, baking powder and ground cloves and, using a metal spoon or plastic spatula, fold it into the egg mixture. When the dry ingredients are almost mixed in, add the nuts and fold in until completely mixed. Press the dough into the tin and brush with the beaten egg. Bake for about 40 minutes, or until golden brown. Remove from the tin, peel off the baking paper and allow to cool on a wire rack.

3 Reduce the oven temperature to very slow 140°C (275°F/Gas 1). When the biscotti are cool, cut into three even-sized pieces, approximately 20 x 6.5 cm (8 x 2¹/2 inches). Cut each piece across the width into pieces approximately 1.5 cm (5/8 inch) wide. Place on a baking tray, cut-side-down, and bake for another 30 minutes, or until the biscotti are golden brown and dry to the touch.

4 Mix the extra sugar with the ground cloves on a tray or a large piece of greaseproof paper. Remove the biscotti from the tray and roll in the flavoured sugar.

Chef's tips To roast the hazelnuts and almonds, place on a baking tray and roast in a moderate oven 180°C (350°F/Gas 4) for 3–5 minutes, taking care not to let the nuts burn.

For a variation, add 100 g (3¹/4 oz) chopped dried apricots and substitute ¹/2 teaspoon ground cinnamon for the ground cloves.

Honey wafers

These deliciously crispy and light biscuits are ideal to use as an accompaniment for a scoop of vanilla ice cream or a fresh fruit sorbet.

*Preparation time **10 minutes + 15 minutes refrigeration***
*Total cooking time **3 minutes per tray***
Makes about 30

30 g (1 oz) unsalted butter, at room temperature
35 g (1 1/4 oz) icing sugar
60 g (2 oz) honey
40 g (1 1/4 oz) plain flour
large pinch of salt
1 teaspoon ground cinnamon

1 Preheat the oven to very hot 230°C (450°F/Gas 8). Brush two baking trays with melted butter and refrigerate.
2 Using a wooden spoon or an electric whisk, cream the butter and icing sugar until light and fluffy. Beat in the honey until thoroughly mixed in. Sift together the flour, salt and cinnamon and stir into the butter mixture.

Cover the bowl with plastic wrap and refrigerate for about 15 minutes before using.
3 Cut a piece of thick cardboard or plastic to about 6 cm (21/2 inches) square. Cut a circle 5 cm (2 inches) in diameter from the centre of the square to make a stencil. Prepare the biscuits with the cardboard or plastic stencil, following the method in the Chef's techniques on page 62. Refrigerate the remaining mixture.
4 Bake for 2–3 minutes, or until golden brown. Using a palette knife or a fish slice, lift the wafers from the tray while still hot. If the wafers set before you can remove them all from the baking tray, return them to the oven to warm slightly. Cool on a wire rack. Repeat with the remaining mixture, preparing the trays as instructed in step 1. Store in an airtight container.

Chef's tip These biscuits become soft very quickly, so eat as soon as possible after baking.

Viennese fingers

These wonderful chocolate-dipped biscuits simply melt in the mouth.

Preparation time **25 minutes**
Total cooking time **10 minutes per tray**
Makes 16

120 g (4 oz) unsalted butter, at room temperature
2–3 drops vanilla extract or essence
1 teaspoon finely grated lemon rind
50 g (1³/4 oz) icing sugar
1 egg, lightly beaten
150 g (5 oz) plain flour
200 g (6¹/2 oz) dark chocolate

1 Brush two baking trays with melted butter and refrigerate. Preheat the oven to moderately hot 200°C (400°F/Gas 6).
2 Using a wooden spoon or electric whisk, cream the butter, vanilla, lemon rind and icing sugar until light and fluffy. Gradually add the egg, a little at a time, beating well after each addition. Sift in the flour and stir to mix.
3 Spoon the mixture into a piping bag with a 1 cm (¹/2 inch) star nozzle. Pipe enough 6–8 cm (2¹/2–3 inch) lengths to fill the prepared baking trays, spacing them slightly apart. Bake for 7–10 minutes, or until golden brown. Cool on a wire rack. Repeat with the remaining mixture, preparing the cooled trays as instructed in step 1.
4 Half-fill a pan with water and bring to the boil. Remove from the heat, place the chocolate in a heatproof bowl and set over the steaming water. Stir until the chocolate melts. Dip one end of each biscuit in the chocolate and cool on a tray covered with baking paper.

Chef's tip For a variation, pipe the biscuits into rosettes about 4 cm (1¹/2 inches) wide (see Chef's techniques, page 63). When cooked, divide into pairs. Spread the bottom of one with some jam, then stick the two together. Dust with icing sugar and place in paper cases.

Brandy snaps with pistachio cream

These crisp, lacy, rolled biscuits are often served in England filled with brandy-flavoured whipped cream. Here, they are filled with pistachio cream, but they are also delicious served plain or dipped in chocolate.

Preparation time **25 minutes + 30 minutes refrigeration**
Total cooking time **15 minutes per tray**
Makes 32

65 g (2¼ oz) unsalted butter
60 g (2 oz) light brown sugar or demerara
55 g (1¾ oz) golden syrup
60 g (2 oz) plain flour
small pinch of ground ginger
50 g (1¾ oz) shelled pistachios
150 ml (5 fl oz) cream, for whipping

1 Brush two baking trays with melted butter.
2 Place the butter, sugar and golden syrup in a small saucepan. Stir gently over low heat until the sugar has dissolved. Cool for 1 minute. Sift the flour with the ginger and stir into the mixture, mixing well.
3 Transfer the mixture to a bowl and refrigerate for 30 minutes, or until it has cooled and is firm. Preheat the oven to moderate 180°C (350°F/Gas 4). Drop enough teaspoons of the mixture in small rounds to fill the prepared baking trays, spacing them at least 10 cm (4 inches) apart. Press down with the spoon to flatten slightly, and bake the brandy snaps for 5–6 minutes, or

until golden brown (see Chef's techniques, page 62).
4 Immediately loosen the brandy snaps from the tray using a spatula and, working quickly, shape them around the handle of a wooden spoon (see Chef's techniques, page 62). If they begin to set before you have finished shaping, return them to the oven briefly to warm. Repeat with the remaining mixture, preparing the trays as instructed in step 1. Warm the mixture a little if it has cooled too much to spoon easily.
5 Bring a small saucepan of water to the boil. Add the pistachios, simmer for 5 minutes, then drain. Transfer to a bowl of cold water and pop them out of their skins by pressing them between your finger and thumb. Chop roughly and brown them under a preheated grill for 1–2 minutes. Cool, then grind a third of the nuts into a paste in a pestle and mortar, blender or food processor. Lightly whip the cream, fold in the ground nuts, then spoon into a piping bag fitted with a small star or plain nozzle and carefully pipe into both ends of the brandy snaps. Decorate the ends with the chopped pistachios.

Chef's tips The unfilled brandy snaps can be stored in an airtight container in a cool, dry place for a few days.

Make very small brandy snaps to serve as petits fours with coffee at the end of a meal.

Quick oatmeal cookies

A chewy and buttery cookie, with a hint of orange and vanilla, to which you can add nuts, chocolate chips and sunflower seeds.

Preparation time **15 minutes**
Total cooking time **12 minutes per tray**
Makes about 36

125 g (4 oz) plain flour
1/2 teaspoon bicarbonate of soda
1/2 teaspoon baking powder
1/2 teaspoon salt
100 g (3 1/4 oz) brown sugar
125 g (4 oz) sugar
125 g (4 oz) unsalted butter
1 egg, lightly beaten
1 teaspoon vanilla extract or essence
1 tablespoon milk
1 teaspoon finely grated orange rind
160 g (5 1/4 oz) rolled oats
125 g (4 oz) raisins

1 Preheat the oven to moderate 180°C (350°F/Gas 4). Line two baking trays with baking paper. Sift together the flour, bicarbonate of soda, baking powder and salt.
2 Cream together the sugars and butter. Add the egg, vanilla and milk, and beat until smooth. Stir in the sifted ingredients and mix well. Stir in the grated orange rind, then the oats and raisins.
3 Scoop up balls of the dough with a tablespoon and drop enough of them to fill the prepared baking trays, spacing them approximately 5 cm (2 inches) apart (see Chef's techniques, page 63). Bake for 10–12 minutes, or until just brown. Remove immediately from the baking trays and cool on a wire rack. Repeat with the remaining mixture, preparing the trays as instructed in step 1.

Chef's tip If you are cooking more than one tray of biscuits in a non-convection oven, swap them around halfway through cooking to ensure even baking.

Fours pochés

In French a 'poche' may refer to a piping bag, hence the name of these petits fours biscuits that are piped onto baking trays before being topped with either a cherry, almond or hazelnut.

*Preparation time **10 minutes + 30 minutes resting***
*Total cooking time **15 minutes***
Makes 16–18

135 g (4¹/2 oz) ground almonds
90 g (3 oz) caster sugar
2 small egg whites
2 teaspoons apricot jam, sieved
2 drops vanilla extract or essence
2 drops almond essence
almonds halves, for decoration
glacé cherry halves, for decoration
whole hazelnuts, for decoration

1 Preheat the oven to moderate 180°C (350°F/Gas 4). Line two baking trays with baking paper. Sift the ground almonds and sugar twice and place in a bowl with one of the egg whites, the apricot jam, vanilla and almond essence. Stir together and add just enough of the remaining egg white to give a firm consistency—the mixture should be almost too thick to pipe.

2 Spoon the mixture into a piping bag fitted with a 1 cm (1/2 inch) star nozzle and pipe 4 cm (11/2 inch) rosettes onto the paper (see Chef's techniques, page 63). Decorate the top of each rosette with either a half almond, half glacé cherry or whole hazelnut. Leave to stand at room temperature for 30 minutes.

3 Bake the biscuits for 15 minutes, or until golden brown, but not too dark. Transfer to a wire rack to cool.

Chef's tips These biscuits will keep in an airtight container for up to 2 weeks.

If you are cooking more than one tray of biscuits in a non-convection oven, swap them around halfway through cooking to ensure even baking.

Snickerdoodles

These citrus-flavoured biscuits with their cinnamon sugar coating have appeared under many different names in regional American cookbooks since the last century. In many midwest cookbooks they are referred to as Snickerdoodles, as in this recipe.

Preparation time **15 minutes + 30 minutes chilling**
Total cooking time **12 minutes per tray**
Makes about 30

250 g (8 oz) plain flour
1/2 teaspoon bicarbonate of soda
1/4 teaspoon salt
large pinch of grated nutmeg
115 g (3³/4 oz) unsalted butter, at room temperature
175 g (5³/4 oz) sugar
1 egg
1 egg yolk
1 teaspoon vanilla extract or essence
1 teaspoon finely grated lemon or orange rind
2 teaspoons ground cinnamon, to coat
2 tablespoons sugar, to coat

1 Preheat the oven to moderately hot 190°C (375°F/Gas 5). Prepare two baking trays by brushing with melted butter.

2 Sift together the flour, bicarbonate of soda, salt and grated nutmeg. Cream together the butter and sugar, add the egg, egg yolk, vanilla and lemon or orange rind. Beat until light and fluffy. Add the sifted ingredients and mix well. Scrape down the sides, cover the bowl with a piece of plastic wrap and refrigerate for 30 minutes. Mix the cinnamon and sugar together in a small bowl.

3 Using a teaspoon, scoop up small amounts of the dough and roll them into balls about 2.5 cm (1 inch) in diameter. Roll the balls in the cinnamon sugar and use enough to fill the prepared baking trays, spacing about 5 cm (2 inches) apart. Slightly flatten the balls and bake for about 12 minutes, or until the biscuits are just starting to brown around the edges and slide easily from the baking tray. Remove from the baking tray and cool on a wire rack. Repeat with the remaining mixture, preparing the trays as instructed in step 1.

Chef's tip If you are cooking more than one tray of biscuits in a non-convection oven, swap them around halfway through cooking to ensure even baking.

Gingernuts

The tantalizing spicy aroma of these biscuits as they come out of the oven is bound to test your willpower. It will be difficult to wait for them to cool and become hard and crunchy as they should be.

Preparation time **15 minutes + 1 hour 30 minutes**
    refrigeration
Total cooking time **15 minutes per tray**
Makes about 40

70 g (2¹/4 oz) unsalted butter, at room temperature
200 g (6¹/2 oz) sugar
I egg
70 g (2¹/4 oz) treacle
2 teaspoons white wine vinegar
240 g (7¹/2 oz) strong or plain flour
1¹/2 teaspoons bicarbonate of soda
¹/2 teaspoon ground ginger
pinch ground cinnamon
pinch of ground cloves
pinch of ground cardamom
sugar, to coat

1 Preheat the oven to moderately hot 190°C (375°F/Gas 5). Line two baking trays with baking paper.
2 Using a wooden spoon or an electric whisk, cream together the butter and sugar until light and fluffy. Add the egg, a little at a time, beating well after each addition, then add the treacle and vinegar and mix well.
3 Sift together the flour, bicarbonate of soda, ground ginger, cinnamon, cloves and cardamom and stir into the butter mixture. Draw a ball of dough together with your hands, wrap it in plastic wrap and refrigerate for about 1 1/2 hours, or until firm.
4 Divide the dough into four and, using the palms of your hands, roll each piece into a rope. Cut each rope into 10 pieces and roll the pieces into balls. Spread the sugar in a shallow tray. Roll each ball through the sugar, place on the prepared trays spaced well apart and press down slightly to flatten. Refrigerate the remaining dough until needed. Bake for about 10–15 minutes, or until golden brown. Repeat with the remaining mixture, preparing the trays as instructed in step 1.

Chef's tips This biscuit dough can be prepared in advance, rolled in the sugar and slightly flattened. Wrap in plastic wrap and freeze as individual pieces. To cook, place the frozen balls on a lined baking tray and bake at moderately hot 190°C (375°F/Gas 5) for 20 minutes.

If you are cooking more than one tray of biscuits in a non-convection oven, swap them around halfway through cooking to ensure even baking.

Paintbox cookies

Buy a variety of different sized paintbrushes and the cookies become your canvas.

Preparation time **25 minutes + 1 hour refrigeration**
Total cooking time **12 minutes per tray**
Makes about 36

300 g (10 oz) unsalted butter, at room temperature
375 g (12 oz) caster sugar
2 eggs
2 teaspoons vanilla extract or essence
375 g (12 oz) plain flour
1/2 teaspoon bicarbonate of soda
1 teaspoon salt
4 egg yolks
4 types of food colouring

1 Preheat the oven to moderate 180°C (350°F/Gas 4). Brush two baking trays with melted butter.

2 Cream the butter and sugar until light and fluffy. Add the eggs and vanilla and stir well. Sift the flour, bicarbonate of soda and salt into the mixture and combine. Wrap the dough in plastic wrap and refrigerate for about 1 hour, or until firm. If it becomes too hard, leave at room temperature for about 20 minutes.

3 Place each egg yolk in a separate bowl. Add a teaspoon of water and beat well with a fork. Add a few drops of a different food colour to each one.

4 Divide the dough in two, keep half refrigerated and roll out the other half between two sheets of baking paper to about a 3–4 mm (1/8–1/4 inch) thickness (see Chef's techniques, pages 63). Cut out shapes and use enough to fill the prepared baking trays. Use small paintbrushes to paint the cookies, adding a little extra water to the food colourings to create a more translucent effect. Allow the 'paint' to dry before baking.

5 Bake for 10–12 minutes, or until lightly coloured. Cool on a wire rack. Repeat with the remaining mixture, preparing the trays as instructed in step 1.

Peanut butter cookies

Peanut butter, the spread made from ground roasted peanuts, is a favourite for many—children and adults alike. Is it any wonder then that these cookies are so popular?

*Preparation time **20 minutes + 1 hour refrigeration***
*Total cooking time **15 minutes per tray***
Makes 30

120 g (4 oz) unsalted butter, at room temperature
120 g (4 oz) sugar
80 g (2³/4 oz) soft brown sugar
1 teaspoon vanilla extract or essence
125 g (4 oz) crunchy peanut butter
1 egg, lightly beaten
175 g (5³/4 oz) strong or plain flour
2 teaspoons baking powder
small pinch of salt
75 g (2¹/2 oz) unsalted peanuts, chopped and roasted (see Chef's tips)
100 g (3¹/4 oz) unsalted peanuts, to garnish

1 Line two baking trays with baking paper. Using electric beaters, cream together the butter and sugars until light and fluffy. Add the vanilla and peanut butter and mix well.

2 Gradually add the egg, a little at a time, beating well after each addition. Sift the flour, baking powder and salt together, add to the butter mixture and mix well.

Stir in the chopped peanuts. Scrape the mixture out of the bowl onto a large piece of plastic wrap, cover and refrigerate for about 1 hour, or until firm.

3 Divide the dough into three pieces. On a floured surface, roll each third into a rope. Cut each rope into 10 equal-sized pieces. Preheat the oven to moderate 180°C (350°F/Gas 4).

4 Roll each piece of dough in your hands to form a smooth ball, then use enough balls of dough to fill the two prepared baking trays, spacing the biscuits well apart. Flatten slightly using a fork (if you find the dough sticks to the fork, dip the fork into a little flour). Arrange three peanuts on top of each biscuit, then place in the oven to bake for about 12–15 minutes, or until golden brown. Transfer to a wire rack to cool. Repeat with the remaining mixture, preparing the trays as in step 1.

Chef's tips Once rolled into ropes, this dough can be stored in the freezer for up to 1 month.

To roast the peanuts, place on a baking tray and roast in a moderate oven 180°C (350°F/Gas 4) for about 2–3 minutes, taking care not to let the nuts burn.

For a variation, add 50 g (1³/4 oz) dark chocolate chips or replace the roasted chopped peanuts with roasted chopped hazelnuts.

Christmas biscuits

These little biscuits with their jewel-like pieces of fruit are extremely popular. Carefully arranged in decorative boxes, they make ideal Christmas presents.

Preparation time **25 minutes + 20 minutes refrigeration**
Total cooking time **10 minutes**
Makes 12

150 g (5 oz) unsalted butter, at room temperature
150 g (5 oz) caster sugar
1 egg, beaten
finely grated rind of 1/2 lemon
finely grated rind of 1/2 orange
50 g (1 3/4 oz) angelica or green glacé
  cherries, chopped
50 g (1 3/4 oz) red glacé cherries, chopped
50 g (1 3/4 oz) chopped mixed peel
250 g (8 oz) plain flour
1/2 teaspoon ground mace
1/2 teaspoon ground cinnamon
1/2 teaspoon ground cloves
1/2 teaspoon ground nutmeg

1 Preheat the oven to moderate 180°C (350°F/Gas 4). Brush two baking trays with melted butter and refrigerate.
2 Using a wooden spoon or electric beaters, cream together the butter and sugar. Gradually add the egg, beating well after each addition. Mix in the lemon and orange rind, angelica or green glacé cherries, red glacé cherries and mixed peel.

3 Sift the flour and ground spices into the mixture and combine. Using a plastic spatula, scrape on to a piece of plastic wrap and flatten lightly with your hand. Wrap in plastic wrap and refrigerate for 20 minutes until firm.
4 Place the dough between two sheets of baking paper and roll out to a 3 mm (1/8 inch) thickness (see Chef's techniques, page 63). Cut out biscuits using some 5 cm (2 inch) decorative cutters and place them on the prepared baking trays, spacing slightly apart. Prick each one with a fork several times and bake for 10 minutes, or until just golden brown and firm to the touch. Cool for 1 minute on the tray, then using a palette knife, lift them onto a wire rack to cool.

Chef's tips Store these biscuits in an airtight container. Placing a piece of white bread in the container will prevent them from becoming stale.

For a variation, lightly beat 1 egg white and add enough sifted icing sugar to form a very stiff paste. Spread a little icing onto each biscuit and top with toasted flaked nuts or glacé cherries before baking. You could also change the spices from mixed spice to just one spice, such as cinnamon.

Chef's techniques

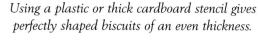

Making brandy snaps

Brandy snaps need to be shaped while hot. If they harden up, put them back in the oven for 30 seconds.

Press a level teaspoon of the mixture down with a spoon to flatten slightly.

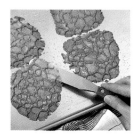

When the brandy snaps come out of the oven, loosen them from the baking tray immediately using a spatula.

Working quickly while they are warm, shape them around the handle of a wooden spoon

Using a stencil

Using a plastic or thick cardboard stencil gives perfectly shaped biscuits of an even thickness.

Place the stencil on a prepared baking tray and spoon a little mixture into the hole.

Level off the mixture using a palette knife

Remove the stencil carefully and repeat with enough of the mixture to fill the prepared baking trays, spacing the biscuits well apart.

When cooked, immediately remove the biscuits from the tray while still warm and pliable.

Making tuiles

Tuiles need to be shaped while still warm. Using a rolling pin gives the biscuits their classic shape.

Drop a level teaspoon of the mixture onto a tray and flatten slightly with a spoon.

Using a wet fork, evenly spread the mixture out so that it is very thin.

Remove the tuiles from the tray while still hot and place on a rolling pin to shape. Transfer to a wire rack to cool.

Rolling and cutting dough

Rolling the dough gives an even thickness and colouring in baking and a professional finish.

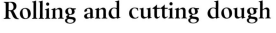

Roll out the biscuit dough between two sheets of baking paper.

Remove the baking paper and cut out the biscuits using shaped cutters. Place on the prepared baking tray.

Piped biscuits

Piping biscuits gives them an even size and a neat appearance.

Pipe rosettes onto the prepared baking tray, spacing them well apart.

Dropped biscuits

The dough for dropped biscuits needs to be soft enough to fall from the spoon.

Scoop up balls of dough with a tablespoon and drop them onto the prepared baking tray.

Published by Murdoch Books® a division of Murdoch Magazines Pty Limited, 45 Jones Street, Ultimo NSW 2007.

Murdoch Books and Le Cordon Bleu thank the 32 masterchefs of all the Le Cordon Bleu Schools, whose knowledge and expertise have made this book possible, especially: Chef Cliche (MOF), Chef Terrien, Chef Boucheret, Chef Duchêne (MOF), Chef Guillut, Chef Steneck, Paris; Chef Males, Chef Walsh, Chef Hardy, London; Chef Chantefort, Chef Bertin, Chef Jambert, Chef Honda, Tokyo; Chef Salembien, Chef Boutin, Chef Harris, Sydney; Chef Lawes, Adelaide; Chef Guiet, Chef Denis, Ottawa. Of the many students who helped the Chefs test each recipe, a special mention to graduates David Welch and Allen Wertheim. A very special acknowledgment to Directors Susan Eckstein, Great Britain, and Kathy Shaw, Paris, who have been responsible for the coordination of the Le Cordon Bleu team throughout this series.

Murdoch Books®
Managing Editor: Kay Halsey
Series Concept, Design and Art Direction: Juliet Cohen
Editor: Elizabeth Cotton
Food Director: Jody Vassallo
Food Editors: Lulu Grimes, Tracy Rutherford
Designer: Norman Baptista
Photographer: Luis Martin
Food Stylist: Rosemary Mellish
Food Preparation: Tracey Port
Chef's Techniques Photographer: Reg Morrison
Home Economists: Michelle Lawton, Kerrie Mullins, Tracey Port, Kerrie Ray

CEO & Publisher: Anne Wilson
Publishing Director: Catie Ziller
General Manager: Mark Smith
Creative Director: Marylouise Brammer
International Sales Director: Mark Newman

National Library of Australia Cataloguing-in-Publication Data
Biscuits. ISBN 0 86411 746 9. 1. Biscuits. 2. Baking. (Series: Le Cordon Bleu home collection). 641.8654

Printed by Toppan Printing (S) Pte. Ltd.
First Printed 1998
©Design and photography Murdoch Books® 1998
©Text Le Cordon Bleu 1998
Distributed in the UK by D Services, 6 Euston Street, Freemen's Common, Leicester LE2 7SS Tel 0116-254-7671 Fax 0116-254-4670. Distributed in Canada by Whitecap (Vancouver) Ltd, 351 Lynn Avenue, North Vancouver, BC V7J 2C4 Tel 604-980-9852 Fax 604-980-8197 or Whitecap (Ontario) Ltd, 47 Coldwater Road, North York, ON M3B 1Y8 Tel 416-444-3442 Fax 416-444-6630

The Publisher and Le Cordon Bleu wish to thank Carole Sweetnam for her help with this series.
Front cover: Macaroons

IMPORTANT INFORMATION

CONVERSION GUIDE

1 cup = 250 ml (8 fl oz)
1 Australian tablespoon = 20 ml (4 teaspoons)
1 UK tablespoon = 15 ml (3 teaspoons)

NOTE: We have used 20 ml tablespoons. If you are using a 15 ml tablespoon, for most recipes the difference will be negligible. For recipes using baking powder, gelatine, bicarbonate of soda and flour, add an extra teaspoon for each tablespoon specified.

CUP CONVERSIONS—DRY INGREDIENTS

1 cup flour, plain or self-raising = 125 g (4 oz)
1 cup sugar, caster = 250 g (8 oz)
1 cup breadcrumbs, dry = 125 g (4 oz)

IMPORTANT: Those who might be at risk from the effects of salmonella food poisoning (the elderly, pregnant women, young children and those suffering from immune deficiency diseases) should consult their GP with any concerns about eating raw eggs.